HONOR GOD WITH YOUR LIFE

WORKBOOK

TIFFANY PURIFOY

Honor God With Your Life Workbook

Copyright © 2021 by Tiffany Purifoy

All rights reserved. No part of this workbook may be reproduced or transmitted in any form or by any means, electronic or mechanical, including photocopying, recording, or by an information storage and retrieval system - except by a reviewer who may quote brief passages in a review to be printed in a magazine or newspaper - without permission in writing from the publisher.

Scripture quotations marked (KJV) are taken from the King James Version of the Bible, public domain.

Scripture quotations marked (AMP) are taken from the Amplified Bible, copyright © 1954, 1958, 1962, 1964, 1965, 1987 by The Lockman Foundation Used by permission." (www.Lockman.org)

Scripture quotations marked (NLT) are taken from the Holy Bible, New Living Translation, copyright 1996, 2004, 2007 by Tyndale House Foundation. Used by permission of Tyndale House Publishers, Inc., Carol Stream, Illinois 60188. All rights reserved.

Scripture quotations marked (MSG) are taken from THE MESSAGE, copyright © 1993, 2002, 2018 by Eugene H. Peterson. Used by permission of NavPress. All rights reserved. Represented by Tyndale House Publishers, Inc.

Scripture quotations marked (NKJV) are taken from the New King James Version ®. Copyright © 1982 by Thomas Nelson. Used by permission. All rights reserved.

Scripture quotations marked (TLB) are taken from The Living Bible copyright © 1971. Used by permission of Tyndale House Publishers, Inc., Carol Stream, Illinois 60188. All rights reserved.
ISBN: 978-1-731-34856-2

Scripture quotations marked (NIV) are taken from the Holy Bible, New International Version®, NIV®. Copyright © 1973, 1978, 1984, 2011 by Biblica, Inc.™ Used by permission of Zondervan. All rights reserved worldwide. www.zondervan.comThe "NIV" and "New International Version" are trademarks registered in the United States Patent and Trademark Office by Biblica, Inc.™

ISBN: 9798706072650

CONTENTS

Chapter 1	Embrace God's Plan	1
Chapter 2	Have Confidence in God	13
Chapter 3	See the Lord as Your Shepherd	23
Chapter 4	Love	33
Chapter 5	Study God's Word	41
Chapter 6	Manage Your Thoughts	51
Chapter 7	Develop an A-W-E-S-O-M-E Prayer Life	59
Chapter 8	Practice Discipline and Diligence	67
Chapter 9	Maintain Your God-Given Authority	73
Chapter 10	Know Him for Yourself	91

Dear Reader,

Thank you very much for choosing this workbook. It accompanies the book, Honor God with Your Life, and is designed to help you dig deeper by applying the principles discussed in each chapter.

If you take the time to read the chapters, study the scriptures, and complete the exercises in this workbook, you will see amazing results in your life. I know this is true, because these are the very same principles I have used in my own life, and I continue to do so to this very day.

This workbook is designed to be used both individually and in groups. You can complete the exercises on your own, then connect with others and share your insights. You'll be surprised at how much more impactful your experience will be when you choose to collaborate with others.

I hope you enjoy both the book and workbook and I look forward to hearing from you soon!

Sincerely,

Tiffany Puriboy

Chapter 1

Embrace God's Plans

Transformation

Don't copy the behavior and customs of this world, but be a new and different person with a fresh newness in all you do and think. Then you will learn from your own experience how His ways will really satisfy you.

Romans 12:2, TLB

Chapter 1

Embrace God's Plans

What are God's plans for me?

Love	John 3:16
Eternal life	John 3:16
Abundant life	John 10:10
Peace and well-being	Jeremiah 29:11, Proverbs 16:3
Hope	Jeremiah 29:11
A promising future	Jeremiah 29:11
Provision	Philippians 4:19
Exceeded expectations	Ephesians 3:20
To not harm me	Jeremiah 29:11
To help me	Psalm 121:1
To teach me	John 14:6
To not condemn me	Romans 8:1

How God's plans are making a difference in my life.....

Chapter 1

Embrace God's Plan

Developing a growth mindset requires recognizing the opportunity to learn from both good and bad situations. What "sunlight" and "rain" experiences have you encountered and what lessons have they taught you? How have those lessons contributed to your personal and spiritual growth?

Some of my joyful experiences (sunlight) have been....

Some of my not-so-pleasant experiences (rain) have been....

Lessons I have learned include...

Those lessons helped me grow in the following ways:

And I am sure that God who began the good work within you will keep right on helping you grow in His grace until His task within you is finally finished on that day when Jesus Christ returns. Philippians 1:6, TLB

HONOR GOD WITH YOUR LIFE WORKBOOK

Chapter 1

Embrace God's Plan

Reflecting His Nature

The Bible tells us that God created us in His image and after His likeness, but because of the sin that entered the world through disobedience, we are born with a sinful nature. Therefore, according to the Bible in John 3, Jesus said we must be born again. We must be born spiritually, so that we can experience life the way God originally intended. Only through our spiritual nature can we develop spiritual qualities, which reflect God's image and His likeness. Because we exist to have both natural and spiritual experiences, we will be confronted with what the Bible refers to as works of the flesh. But to live the way God intended, our goal should always be to be fruitful, multiply, replenish the earth, and subdue it (Genesis 1:28). When we produce spiritual fruit as found in Galatians 5:22-23, and when we multiply that fruit through continuous nurturing of the spiritual seeds we plant, we will replenish the earth with that fruit, and we'll be able to overcome the works of the flesh.

Chapter 1

Embrace God's Plan

Read Galatians 5:16-26
Then list the fruit of the spirit (See verses 22-23) and works of the flesh (See verses 19-21) below.

FRUIT OF THE SPIRIT

Producing this
in my life...

WORKS OF THE FLESH

...gives me the power
to overcome this!

Chapter 1

Embrace God's Plan

As we walk with God and learn more about Him through His Word, we'll discover that that there are some things we need to let go of, because they're not adding any value to our lives. Some examples include:

- Old thought patterns
- A defeated mentality
- Destructive habits
- Wrong influences

Things I need to let go of:

Chapter 1

Embrace God's Plan

> God is Spirit, and those who worship Him must worship in spirit and in truth.
>
> John 4:24, NKJV

Chapter 1

Embrace God's Plan

Notes

Chapter 1

Embrace God's Plan

Notes

Chapter 1

Embrace God's Plan

Notes

Chapter 1

Embrace God's Plan

Notes

Chapter 2

Have Confidence in God

Confidence

Trust in the Lord with all your heart; do not depend on your own understanding. Seek His will in all you do, and He will show you which path to take.

Proverbs 3:5-6, NLT

Chapter 2

Have Confidence in God

Take a moment to write down your goals.
On a scale of 1 to 10, rank your current level of confidence in seeing them fulfilled,
1 = least and 10 = greatest

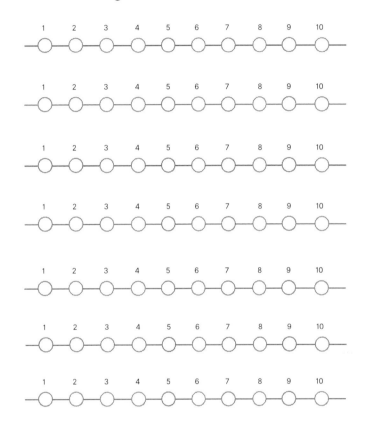

NOTES

Chapter 2

Have Confidence in God

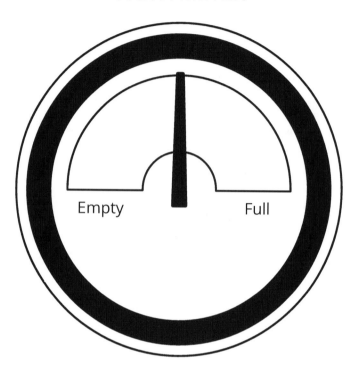

FAITH METER

Empty   Full

How much faith do you think you have that God will answer your prayers?

I can fill my faith meter by.....

HONOR GOD WITH YOUR LIFE WORKBOOK

Chapter 2

Have Confidence in God

Persistence

The key to getting results is first deciding what you really want and then being willing to persist despite any obstacles you face. Some people mistakenly believe that opposition is a sign that something they want is just not meant for them. On the contrary, it could be an indicator that you are on the right track, and that you need to persevere through the challenges. Those hurdles are there to test your commitment to whatever it is that you are trying to achieve.

Anything worth having will require some level of determination and follow through. Do not give up just because something appears to be too difficult, complicated, or inconvenient. Breakthrough and overflow are waiting on the other side of your persistence.

Areas I can be more persistent in:

Chapter 2

Have Confidence in God

> But David encouraged himself in the Lord his God.
>
> 1 Samuel 30:6, KJV

Chapter 2
Have Confidence in God

Notes

Chapter 2

Have Confidence in God

Notes

Chapter 2
Have Confidence in God

Notes

Chapter 2

Have Confidence in God

Notes

Chapter 3

See the Lord as Your Shepherd

Guidance

The Lord is my Shepherd.
I have all that I need.

Psalm 23:1, NLT

Chapter 3

See the Lord as Your Shepherd

Read Psalm 23.

Think about the things you're trusting and believing God to help you with.

List them under each category.

Provision

_____
_____
_____
_____
_____
_____
_____

Rest

_____
_____
_____
_____
_____
_____
_____

Direction

_____
_____
_____
_____
_____
_____
_____

Restoration

_____
_____
_____
_____
_____
_____
_____

Chapter 3

See the Lord as Your Shepherd

Continued

Decision-making

_____
_____
_____
_____
_____
_____
_____
_____

Safety & Security

_____
_____
_____
_____
_____
_____
_____
_____

Blessings Overflowing

_____
_____
_____
_____
_____
_____
_____
_____

Compassion & Forgiveness

_____
_____
_____
_____
_____
_____
_____
_____

Chapter 3

See the Lord as Your Shepherd

Trusting God to provide direction when the path ahead is unclear can seem difficult at times. But when you take out the time to seek Him for guidance, you'll begin to recognize whether your plans and decisions are aligned with His will.

I am seeking God's guidance in this area:

My current plans and decisions:

Is my current plan morally right?

Does it honor God?

Who will my decisions impact and in what way?

Chapter 3

See the Lord as Your Shepherd

Do not fear, for I am with you.

Do not be dismayed, for I am your God.

I will strengthen you and help you.

I will uphold you

with my righteous right hand.

Isaiah 41:10, NIV

Chapter 3

See the Lord as Your Shepherd

Notes

Chapter 3

See the Lord as Your Shepherd

Notes

Chapter 3

See the Lord as Your Shepherd

Notes

Chapter 3

See the Lord as Your Shepherd

Notes

Chapter 4

Love

Love

Most important of all, continue to show deep love for each other, for love covers a multitude of sins.

1 Peter 4:8, NLT

Chapter 4

Love

The Greatest Commandment

You shall Love the Lord your God with all your heart, and with all your soul, and with all your mind. This is the first and greatest commandment. The second is like it. You shall love your neighbor as yourself - that is, unselfishly seek the best or higher good for others. The whole Law and the writings of the Prophets depend on these two commandments. Matthew 22:36-40, AMP

I can demonstrate my love for God by...

I can show love towards others by.....

HONOR GOD WITH YOUR LIFE WORKBOOK

Chapter 4

Love

Too often we spend most of our time caring for and doing for others, only to neglect taking care of ourselves. But if we are running on empty, there will not be much left to give anyone else. For this reason, self-care is extremely important. Remember that love is an action word. Learn to love YOU, knowing that by doing so, you are loving God, who lives within you. When you are at your best, you can give God your best, and you will have a greater capacity to love others.

<u>Self-Care Suggestions</u>
- Get enough rest on a regular basis.
- Plan for and take a nice, enjoyable vacation.
- Go shopping and treat yourself to something nice.
- Spend time getting pampered at the spa.
- Take care of your physical fitness needs.
- Listen to positive, uplifting messages.
- Laugh often.
- Set aside time just for you.
- Take time to enjoy nature.
- Eat well-balanced meals.
- Drink plenty of water.
- Make it a point to have some obligation-free days, evenings, and/or weekends.
- Listen to your favorite music.
- Go for walks.
- Get a new hairstyle.
- Create a playlist of your favorite songs.
- Learn a new skill.
- Take dance lessons.
- Stick with your goals and keep your promises to yourself.
- Say No without feeling guilty.

Highlight or place a checkmark next to the suggestions you will try out. Commit to making your own self-care list.

Chapter 4

Love

Love is patient and kind.

Love is not jealous or boastful or proud or rude.

It does not demand its own way.

It is not irritable,

and it keeps no record of being wronged.

It does not rejoice about injustice but rejoices

whenever the truth wins out.

Love never gives up, never loses faith,

is always hopeful,

and endures through every circumstance.

1 Corinthians 13:4-7, NLT

Chapter 4

Love

My Self-Care List

Chapter 4

Love

My Self-Care List

_____

_____

_____

_____

_____

_____

_____

_____

_____

_____

_____

_____

_____

_____

Chapter 4

Love

Notes

Chapter 5

Study God's Word

Devotion

Keep this Book of the Law always on your lips. Meditate on it day and night, so that you may be careful to do everything written in it. Then you will be prosperous and successful.

Joshua 1:8, NIV

Chapter 5

Study God's Word

Studying God's Word strengthens you spiritually by making you more aware of His presence in your life. It elevates your thinking, strengthens your faith, and causes you to recognize God's intentions for you.

Take some time each day to read and meditate on God's Word. Then write about what comes to mind as you sit silently in His presence, focusing only on His Word.

Chapter 5

Study God's Word

5-Minute Meditation Exercise

Read and meditate on the following scripture for 5 minutes. Alternatively, you can select a scripture of your choice. Then take a few minutes to journal your thoughts for reflection. Repeat this exercise using the same scripture for three consecutive days.

I can do all things through Christ who strengthens me. Philippians 4:13

Day 1

Day 2

Day 3

Chapter 5

Study God's Word

5-Minute Meditation Exercise (Continued)

Read and meditate on the following scripture for 5 minutes. Alternatively, you can select a scripture of your choice. Then take a few minutes to journal your thoughts for reflection. Repeat this exercise using the same scripture for three consecutive days.

You make known to me the path of life; in your presence there is fullness of joy; at your right hand are pleasures forevermore. Psalm 16:11

Day 4

Day 5

Day 6

Chapter 5

Study God's Word

> Blessed Lord, teach me your rules.
>
> I have recited your laws
>
> and rejoiced in them more than in riches.
>
> I will meditate upon them
>
> and give them my full respect.
>
> I will delight in them and not forget them.
>
> Psalm 119:12-16, TLB

Chapter 5

Study God's Word

Notes

Chapter 5

Study God's Word

Notes

Chapter 5

Study God's Word

Notes

Chapter 5

Study God's Word

Notes

Chapter 6

Manage Your Thoughts

Insight

Wisdom is the principal thing. Therefore get wisdom. And in all your getting, get understanding.

Proverbs 4:7, NKJV

Chapter 6

Manage Your Thoughts

Dealing with Distractions

With so much competing for our attention, it is easy to get into the habit of allowing distractions to consume our thoughts and our time. Think about the things that have been a distraction to you recently and consider ways to address them in the future.

Some things that have distracted me recently are....

I could have made better use of my time by...

I plan to address these distractions in the future by...

Chapter 6

Manage Your Thoughts

Positive Thinking

Positivity ignites our creativity, imagination, and ultimately our vision for greater possibilities. But negativity does the exact opposite of that. It stifles us and causes us to develop limited thinking. Take note of the messages and conversations you have seen or heard recently. Consider what types of thoughts and images entered your mind and how they impacted your overall thought process. Make a conscious decision to surround yourself with positivity.

Positive people I enjoy talking to

Uplifting and encouraging TV shows, social media pages, books, and magazines

Negative conversations, TV shows, and social media pages to limit or avoid

Chapter 6

Manage Your Thoughts

Fix your thoughts on what is true, and honorable, and right, and pure, and lovely, and admirable. Think about things that are excellent and worthy of praise.

Philippians 4:8, NLT

Chapter 6
Manage Your Thoughts

Notes

Chapter 6

Manage Your Thoughts

Notes

Chapter 6
Manage Your Thoughts

Notes

Chapter 7

Develop an A-W-E-S-O-M-E Prayer Life

Fervency

The prayer of a person living right with God is something powerful to be reckoned with.

James 5:16, MSG

Chapter 7

Develop and A-W-E-S-O-M-E Prayer Life

7-Day Prayer Challenge

Exercise: Contact a few of your family members and friends and offer to pray for them. Make a list of their names and prayer requests. Pray for the people on your list for seven consecutive days.

Name	Prayer Request

Chapter 7

Develop and A-W-E-S-O-M-E Prayer Life

7-Day Prayer Challenge Follow-Up

Exercise: At the end of the seven days, reach out again to the people you prayed for and ask for any updates on their requests. Refer back to the prayer requests and continue following up with the people on your list. Provide updates as their prayers are answered.

Name	Answered Prayer/Updates

HONOR GOD WITH YOUR LIFE WORKBOOK

Chapter 7

Develop an A-W-E-S-O-M-E Prayer Life

When you pray, go away by yourself,

shut the door behind you,

and pray to your Father in private.

Then your Father,

who sees everything,

will reward you.

Matthew 6:6, NLT

Chapter 7

Develop and A-W-E-S-O-M-E Prayer Life

Notes

Chapter 7
Develop and A-W-E-S-O-M-E Prayer Life

Notes

Chapter 7

Develop and A-W-E-S-O-M-E Prayer Life

Notes

Chapter 8

Practice Discipline and Diligence

Effort

Without faith it is impossible to please God, because anyone who comes to Him must believe that He exists and that He rewards those who earnestly seek Him.

Hebrews 11:6, NIV

Chapter 8

Practice Discipline and Diligence

<u>Tips for improving discipline and diligence:</u>

- Make time with God your priority.
- Develop a habit of getting plenty of rest.
- Establish a routine for doing the things that are important to you.
- Set aside time to plan out your week in advance.
- Wake up earlier to allow more time in the morning for prayer and meditation.
- Schedule a specific time for exercising and make it a weekly routine.
- Limit social media time to allow more time for things with a higher priority.
- Create weekly and/or daily lists for your "to do" items.
- Schedule time for reading and skill development.
- If talking and texting consume your time, limit discussions to create more balance.
- Set goals and get an accountability partner to support you with staying committed.

I can apply more discipline and diligence to these areas of my life:

Chapter 8

Practice Discipline and Diligence

Work hard so God can say to you,

"Well done."

Be a good workman,

one who does not need to be ashamed

when God examines your work.

Know what his Word says and means.

2 Timothy 2:15, TLB

Chapter 8
Practice Discipline and Diligence

Notes

Chapter 8

Practice Discipline and Diligence

Notes

Chapter 9

Maintain Your God-Given Authority

Authority

You will also declare a thing, and it
will be established for you.
So light will shine on your ways.

Job 22:28

Chapter 9

Maintain Your God-Given Authority

Faith affirmations are life-changing ways to achieve desired results by verbally declaring what you want to see happen in your life.

The following pages include some affirmations you can use, or you can choose to create your own.

Chapter 9

Maintain Your God-Given Authority

FAITH AFFIRMATIONS FOR FREEDOM

- I welcome things that will help me to create a positive atmosphere.

- I trust God's guidance as He aligns me with His will.

- I am free from past mistakes and hindrances.

- I look optimistically toward my beautiful bright future.

- I free myself from guilt because of things that I have said and done to hurt others.

- I free those who have hurt and offended me. By freeing them, I now free myself.

- I am free from unforgiveness. I know that I am forgiven. I now commit to forgive myself.

Chapter 9

Maintain Your God-Given Authority

FAITH AFFIRMATIONS FOR DIRECTION

- I am exactly where I need to be at this very moment.

- God is ordering my steps here and now.

- I trust the plans God has for my life. I will experience the hope and future He intends for me.

- As I follow God's direction, I will continue to experience His very best.

- I will not follow in the footsteps of unbelievers, nor seek answers from those who lack wisdom.

HONOR GOD WITH YOUR LIFE WORKBOOK

Chapter 9

Maintain Your God-Given Authority

FAITH AFFIRMATIONS FOR
LOVING THE "ME" GOD CREATED ME TO BE

- I am God's unique creation. He celebrates me, and today I am joining Him in this celebration.

- I am glad to be me. There is no one else I'd rather be.

- Today, I make the decision to look in the mirror and love who I see.

- Every time I see myself, I will smile.

- Every time I think of myself, and all that I am able to accomplish, my heart will be filled with joy.

- Today I make the choice to begin seeing myself the way God sees me.

- I submit myself to God as He continues to mold me into the image of His Son.

- I recognize that I am a person of excellence, because I am God's creation.

Chapter 9

Maintain Your God-Given Authority

FAITH AFFIRMATIONS FOR INTEGRITY

- My heart is in the right place, and I will allow it to guide me every step of the way.

- God is first in my life. Today, I seek Him and desire to be closer to Him than I have ever been.

- I am surrounding myself only with those who have morals, values, character, and integrity.

- My actions are aligned with God's will for my life.

- Today I walk in obedience to God's voice. I will not compromise my values to have my own way.

- My character is in tact. I am a person of high morals and integrity.

Chapter 9

Maintain Your God-Given Authority

FAITH AFFIRMATIONS FOR SUCCESS

- I am making significant progress toward achieving my dreams, goals, and desires.

- I am a successful person, and today I make great things happen in my life.

- My attitude toward life is positive, and I welcome good things to come my way.

- I triumph over every circumstance.

- I am using my God-given ability to succeed.

- The words I speak today will produce great things for me and others.

- I welcome this day into my life as an opportunity to accomplish something remarkable.

- I will exceed my own expectations today.

- I will accomplish something great today.

- Something good is about to happen in my life.

- The decisions I make today produce outstanding results for me and those connected to me.

- I think carefully before speaking, and my words lead to favorable results.

Chapter 9

Maintain Your God-Given Authority

FAITH AFFIRMATIONS FOR
COMPLETION

- I will complete every goal that I have set for my future.

- The work that God has begun in me will be completed at His appointed time.

- Every hindrance that has delayed my progress is being removed.

- Every project that I start will be finished on time.

- Every desire that God has placed within me will be fulfilled.

- My goals will be completed in a timely manner.

Chapter 9
Maintain Your God-Given Authority

FAITH AFFIRMATIONS FOR BUSINESS AND CAREER

- I am an expert in my field.

- I set new standards for others to follow.

- There are no limits to what I can achieve in my business and career.

- My business is prospering and my profits are soaring.

- I can do all things through Christ who strengthens me.

- My business/workplace is the assignment that God has entrusted me with, and I will use this opportunity to help make a difference in other people's lives.

- My life is an example to others that trusting God and living according to His word will always bring about outstanding results.

- I have God's divine favor with me everywhere I go.

Chapter 9

Maintain Your God-Given Authority

FAITH AFFIRMATIONS FOR FORTITUDE

- I use my God-given determination to firmly declare His promises, even in the midst of challenges.

- I will not allow the things I see to change what I believe God can do.

- I am not intimidated by changing circumstances.

- I welcome new opportunities and seize them every chance I get.

- God has not given me a spirit of fear, but of power, love, and a sound mind.

Chapter 9

Maintain Your God-Given Authority

> If you only have faith in God -
>
> this is the absolute truth -
>
> you can say to this Mount of Olives,
>
> 'Rise up and fall into the Mediterranean,'
>
> and your command will be obeyed.
>
> All that's required is that you really believe
>
> and have no doubt!
>
> Listen to me!
>
> You can pray for anything,
>
> and if you believe, you have it, it's yours!
>
> Mark 11: 22-24, TLB

Chapter 9
Maintain Your God-Given Authority

Notes

Chapter 9
Maintain Your God-Given Authority

Notes

Chapter 9

Maintain Your God-Given Authority

Notes

Chapter 9

Maintain Your God-Given Authority

Notes

Chapter 9

Maintain Your God-Given Authority

Notes

Chapter 9
Maintain Your God-Given Authority

Notes

Chapter 10

Know Him for Yourself

Understanding

And we know that Christ, God's Son, has come to help us understand and find the true God. And now we are in God because we are in Jesus Christ his Son, who is the only true God; and he is eternal Life.

1 John 5:20, TLB

Chapter 10

Know Him for Yourself

God elevated Him to the place of highest honor

and gave Him the name above all other names,

that at the name of Jesus every knee should bow,

in heaven and on earth and under the earth,

and every tongue declare that

Jesus Christ is Lord,

to the glory of God the Father.

Philippians 2: 9-11, NLT

Chapter 10

Know Him for Yourself

Names of God

I AM	Exodus 3:14
Jehovah	Exodus 6:3
Jesus	Matthew 1:1, John 1:1-14, John 10:30
Elohim – God of all creation	Genesis 1 and 2
El Elyon – God most high	Genesis 14:18
Adonai – Sovereign Lord, Lord God	Genesis 15:2
El Shaddai – Almighty God	Genesis 17:1
Jehovah Jireh – The Lord will provide	Genesis 22:8-14
Jehovah Rophe – The Lord our Healer	Exodus 15:26
Jehovah Nissi – The Lord our Banner	Exodus 17:15
Jehovah Elokehu – The Lord your God	Exodus 20:2
Jehovah Mekaddishkem – The Lord our Sanctifier	Exodus 31:13
Jehovah Shalom – The Lord our Peace	Judges 6:24
Jehovah Saboath – The Lord of Hosts	1 Samuel 1:3
Jehovah Elyon – The Lord Most High	Psalm 7:17
Jehovah Rohi – The Lord My Shepherd	Psalm 23:1
Jehovah Hoseen – The Lord our Maker	Psalm 95:6
Jehovah Eloheenu – The Lord our God	Psalm 99:5
Emmanuel – God is with us	Isaiah 7:14
Jehovah Tsidkeenu – The Lord our Righteousness	Jeremiah 23:6
Jehovah Shammah – The Lord is Present	Ezekiel 48:35
Jehovah Elohay – The Lord my God	Zechariah 14:5

HONOR GOD WITH YOUR LIFE WORKBOOK

Chapter 10

Know Him for Yourself

Descriptions of God

The Word	John 1:1
Teacher	John 3:2
Light of the world	John 8:12
The Resurrection	John 11:25
Wonderful Counselor	Isaiah 9:6
Mighty God	Isaiah 9:6
Everlasting Father	Isaiah 9:6
Prince of Peace	Isaiah 9:6
Alpha and Omega	Revelations 1:8
King of kings	Revelations 17:14

Name other descriptions of God that are found in the Bible

Chapter 10

Know Him for Yourself

Notes

Notes

Notes

Notes

Notes

Notes

Notes

Notes

Notes

Notes

Notes

Made in the USA
Columbia, SC
25 November 2024

47006233R00061